Who Was
Betsy Ross?

Who Was Betsy Ross?

WITHDRAWN

By James Buckley Jr.
Illustrated by John O'Brien

Grosset & Dunlap
An Imprint of Penguin Group (USA) LLC

For Charlotte and Eleanor, who will someday
be as famous as Betsy Ross!—JB

To Tess, my daughter and favorite Philadelphian!—JOB

GROSSET & DUNLAP
Published by the Penguin Group
Penguin Group (USA) LLC, 375 Hudson Street, New York, New York 10014, USA

USA | Canada | UK | Ireland | Australia | New Zealand | India | South Africa | China

penguin.com
A Penguin Random House Company

Text copyright © 2014 by James Buckley Jr. Illustrations copyright © 2014 by John O'Brien.
Cover illustration copyright © 2014 by Nancy Harrison. All rights reserved. Published by
Grosset & Dunlap, a division of Penguin Young Readers Group, 345 Hudson Street,
New York, New York 10014. GROSSET & DUNLAP is a trademark of
Penguin Group (USA) LLC. Printed in the USA.

Library of Congress Cataloging-in-Publication Data is available.

ISBN 978-0-448-48243-9   10 9 8 7 6 5 4 3 2 1

Contents

Who Was
Betsy Ross?

In the spring of 1764, a young girl in
Philadelphia named Elizabeth Griscom visited her
sister at work. Elizabeth's sister was a seamstress
for an upholstery business. It produced many items
made out of fabric, including curtains, tablecloths,
quilts, sheets, and even cloth-covered furniture.

The workers were kept very busy creating items to decorate some of the most important homes in the American colonies of Great Britain.

Elizabeth, who was known as Betsy, was still in school. Her older sisters were working to help their large family. Betsy knew she would one day join them at the shop.

The morning that Betsy visited the workshop, one of the seamstresses had a problem with a piece of fabric. Betsy was pretty good at sewing. She took a look at the problem and was able to fix it quickly.

John Webster, the owner of the business, saw this and was impressed! Betsy was only twelve, but already she could sew better than some of the older girls.

Webster visited Betsy's mother and asked if Betsy could come work at the shop, too. Mrs. Griscom said yes. A few days later, Betsy's life at school ended and her life as a seamstress began.

Betsy's quick stitching that day was the beginning of a sewing career that lasted almost seventy years. Over time, a legend grew that Betsy herself had sewn something very famous—the first United States flag. That story may or may not be true, but one thing is certain: Betsy Ross and thousands of hardworking women like her helped support the cause of the colonial army and the fight for America's independence.

Chapter 1
A Quaker Girl

The winter of 1752 was one of the worst
Philadelphia had seen. Food was scarce and the
snow was deep. The terrible cold froze animals

as they stood in the fields. In a cabin just outside the city, Betsy Griscom was born on January 1. She joined the large family of Samuel and Rebecca Griscom. Samuel worked in Philadelphia as a carpenter, as his father and grandfather had done. Samuel built homes and furniture for the growing city.

Philadelphia was the largest city in Pennsylvania, one of thirteen colonies in America owned by Great Britain. It was also the largest city in all the American colonies.

People had been coming to America from England for more than one hundred years. In England, they could not always worship how they wanted to. They came to the colonies so that they could follow their own religious traditions. Samuel and Rebecca's parents had made that trip across the Atlantic Ocean. The Griscoms were members of the Society of Friends, a Christian group also known as Quakers.

The Quakers believed in a simple life. They wanted to work, worship, and raise their families. Twice a week, Betsy went to Quaker services with her family. At home, Betsy helped her mother and sisters with many chores, including stacking firewood, sweeping the rooms, and washing dishes.

THE THIRTEEN COLONIES

THE BRITISH CONTROLLED ALL THE LAND ALONG THE ATLANTIC COAST IN THE NEW WORLD OF AMERICA, BUT ENGLAND'S KING GEORGE III GRANTED SPECIFIC PARCELS OF LAND TO PEOPLE WHO WANTED TO COLONIZE—OR SETTLE—IT. ALTHOUGH EACH OF THE THIRTEEN COLONIES HAD ITS OWN HISTORY AND ITS OWN GOVERNOR, THE GOVERNMENT OF THE COLONIES WAS AN EXTENSION OF THE ENGLISH GOVERNMENT.

COLONY	DATE FOUNDED	FOUNDED BY
VIRGINIA	1607	VIRGINIA COMPANY OF LONDON
MASSACHUSETTS	1620	PURITANS
NEW HAMPSHIRE	1623	JOHN MASON
MARYLAND	1632	ROMAN CATHOLICS
CONNECTICUT	1635	VARIOUS PEOPLE
RHODE ISLAND	1636	ROGER WILLIAMS
CAROLINA	1650S	VIRGINIANS
DELAWARE	1664	DUKE OF YORK
NEW YORK	1664	DUKE OF YORK
NEW JERSEY	1664	DUKE OF YORK
PENNSYLVANIA	1682	WILLIAM PENN
GEORGIA	1732	JAMES OGLETHORPE

Quaker children wore very plain clothing. Betsy wore long, dark dresses, usually with long sleeves. And she always wore a bonnet on her head. The older girls sometimes wore mobcaps instead, which looked like small mushrooms.

When Betsy was born, the Griscoms already had five daughters: Deborah, Susannah, Sarah, Rebecca, and Mary. Two other Griscom children had died while infants. Betsy was the eighth child. In time, Betsy's parents would go on to have five more daughters and four sons, all but one of whom died very young. In all, only eight of the Griscoms' seventeen children survived infancy and grew up to be adults.

When Betsy was just a few years old, Samuel moved his family into the bustling city of Philadelphia. He built a large home with eleven rooms for his growing family.

Unlike most religions of the time, Quakers believed both girls and boys should be educated. When Betsy was about six, she started school. She went to a Quaker school run by a teacher named Rebecca Jones.

The students learned to read and do arithmetic. They went to class five days a week,

and then again on Saturday mornings! Along
with their regular lessons, the girls learned how
to sew and make clothing. In the 1700s, most
families made their own clothing.

Betsy learned even more about sewing from her great-aunt Sarah Griscom, who owned her own business making women's corsets.

THE SOCIETY OF FRIENDS

IN THE 1500S AND 1600S, SEVERAL NEW CHRISTIAN MOVEMENTS SPLIT FROM THE LARGER CATHOLIC CHURCH IN EUROPE. AN ENGLISHMAN NAMED GEORGE FOX FOUNDED THE SOCIETY OF FRIENDS, OR QUAKERS. THEY DID AWAY WITH PRIESTS AND SERMONS AND COMMUNION. AND THEY BROKE AWAY FROM THE CHURCH OF ENGLAND. THEY LOOKED TO THEIR "INNER LIGHT" AS THEIR CONNECTION TO GOD. QUAKER SERVICES WERE MOSTLY SILENT. HOWEVER, IF PEOPLE WERE MOVED BY THEIR INNER LIGHT, THEY COULD SPEAK UP ABOUT IT.

GEORGE FOX

LEAVING ENGLAND FOR AMERICA, THE QUAKERS SETTLED MAINLY IN RHODE ISLAND AND PENNSYLVANIA. WILLIAM PENN, A FELLOW QUAKER, HAD FOUNDED PENNSYLVANIA ACCORDING TO THE QUAKER PRINCIPLES. HE ENCOURAGED PEOPLE TO WORSHIP HOWEVER THEY CHOSE. HE NAMED

HIS CAPITAL CITY
PHILADELPHIA, WHICH
MEANS "CITY OF
BROTHERLY LOVE."

WILLIAM PENN

THE QUAKERS ARE
AGAINST ANY KIND OF
WAR OR VIOLENCE.
MANY QUAKERS
REFUSED TO JOIN
THE MILITARY DURING
THE REVOLUTIONARY
WAR; INSTEAD, THEY WORKED TO SUPPORT THE
CAUSE IN OTHER WAYS, SUCH AS SUPPLYING FOOD
AND MEDICAL ASSISTANCE.

THE SOCIETY OF FRIENDS HAS SPLIT INTO MANY
DIFFERENT GROUPS, BUT PEOPLE STILL WORSHIP AS
QUAKERS. TODAY, THE LARGEST GROUPS OF QUAKERS
CAN BE FOUND IN KENYA, GUATEMALA, AND GREAT
BRITAIN.

Chapter 2
Time to Go to Work

Betsy's older sisters all had begun working
when they were teenagers. In the early days of the
American colonies, upholsterers made curtains,

bedcovers, cushions, and pillows. They even made furniture, such as sofas and comfortable chairs. Some upholsterers also made flags.

At this time, Philadelphia was a great place to be an upholsterer. Many of the richest people in the colonies lived there. They had money to spend, and they wanted their homes to be beautiful. They ordered fancy chairs, beautiful tablecloths, and sofas covered with soft velvet imported from Europe.

Some of the workers at John Webster's shop made nothing but fringe and tassels to decorate curtains. The expert craftspeople stitched and sewed for hours to make the finest home furnishings.

Mr. Webster had many helpers. Some were paid workers who had studied and worked their way into a full-time job. Others were apprentices. An *apprentice* is a person who is learning on the job.

They were usually not paid much, if anything, but they hoped to learn enough to one day earn a full-time job.

In 1764, when Betsy was twelve, she visited her sister at Mr. Webster's shop. When Webster saw Betsy's skill, he signed her on as an apprentice. In those days, it was not unusual for children to work outside their homes. Other girls worked in similar shops, or in kitchens or as housemaids. Boys were trained to be printers, carpenters, or sign painters, or to care for horses and carriages.

Betsy worked six days a week. She gathered the materials the workers needed, including fabric, needles, and thread. Sometimes she made deliveries to customers. And she became a better seamstress. She had a busy life in a busy city.

In 1765, Great Britain passed a new tax on its American colonies. This was nothing new, as the colonists were all British subjects and expected to

be loyal to King George III. But this new tax made many colonists angry. The Stamp Act said that every piece of paper had to have a special stamp on it. Those stamps cost the colonists money.

The money was sent back to
England to support the king and
the British army. Americans in
Philadelphia, New York, and Boston
held meetings and protests against
the new taxes. Ordinary citizens like Betsy started
paying attention to the speeches arguing against
Great Britain's rules. In the end, Britain canceled
the Stamp Act. But the American colonists were
growing tired of sending more and more tax
money to Great Britain.

Over the next several years, Betsy continued
working hard for Mr. Webster. The tension
between the American colonies and England grew
worse. But by 1773, Betsy was not paying as much
attention to the politics of her country. She had
fallen in love with another shopworker named
John Ross.

There was only one problem: John Ross was
not a Quaker.

TAXATION WITHOUT REPRESENTATION

WHEN COLONISTS GOT ANGRY BECAUSE OF THE STAMP ACT, THEY WERE NOT MAD ABOUT BEING TAXED. THEY EXPECTED TO PAY TAXES TO HELP RUN THEIR COLONY AND ENGLAND. BUT THE COLONISTS WANTED TO HAVE A SAY ABOUT WHICH TAXES WERE PASSED. PARLIAMENT, THE PART OF ENGLAND'S GOVERNMENT THAT MAKES LAWS, DISAGREED. AND KING GEORGE III, WHO SIGNED ALL THE LAWS, DISAGREED. THEY SAID AMERICANS COULD NOT VOTE ON THEIR OWN TAXES.

KING GEORGE III

A FAMOUS AMERICAN SLOGAN WAS "NO TAXATION WITHOUT REPRESENTATION," BECAUSE THE COLONISTS HAD NO REPRESENTATION IN PARLIAMENT. IN THE LATE 1760S AND EARLY 1770S, ENGLAND IMPOSED MANY OTHER NEW TAXES. AND AMERICANS OBJECTED TO THEM ALL. THE MOST FAMOUS TAX PROTEST WAS THE BOSTON TEA PARTY. IN DECEMBER 1773, PATRIOTS IN BOSTON,

MASSACHUSETTS, DUMPED CHESTS OF ENGLISH TEA INTO BOSTON HARBOR. EVEN THOUGH TEA WAS THEIR FAVORITE DRINK, THEY DID NOT WANT TO PAY TAXES ON IT, AND SO THEY RUINED THE ENTIRE SHIPMENT. THE BOSTON TEA PARTY ANGERED KING GEORGE III AND THE BRITISH GOVERNMENT. LESS THAN TWO YEARS LATER, THE REVOLUTIONARY WAR BEGAN IN AMERICA.

Chapter 3
War!

The Society of Friends did not allow its members to marry people who were not Quakers. They wanted their community to stick together. John was successful. He had opened his own upholstery shop. And he came from a good family. But instead of the Society of Friends, John went to the Church of England. Because of that, Betsy's parents were against her marriage to John.

Betsy and John eloped. They crossed the Delaware River to nearby Gloucester, New Jersey. On November 4, 1773, beside a large wood fireplace at an inn called Hugg's Tavern, they became man and wife.

After her marriage, Betsy was forced to leave the Quakers. They asked her twice to apologize

for marrying Ross, but she refused. She was not
going to say she was sorry that she fell in love.

Betsy joined John's church, Christ Church on Second Street in Philadelphia. She left Mr. Webster's shop and began working alongside John.

CHRIST CHURCH

Betsy and John started their married life at a very exciting time in Philadelphia. The anger in America over the tea tax and other insults was growing. Citizens wanted to band together to force a change. In the summer of 1774, colonial leaders gathered in Philadelphia. They came from the other colonies to plan their next move.

In fact, these men wanted America to split from Great Britain and form an independent country. To take the steps toward independence, they met at the Continental Congress; it was the first time that leaders from each colony had come together to discuss their dreams for a new nation. The Congress sent a letter to King George, demanding the right to "life, liberty, and property."

COLONIAL GOVERNMENT

EACH OF THE THIRTEEN COLONIES WAS FORMED BY DIFFERENT GROUPS OF SETTLERS. THEY CHOSE DIFFERENT WAYS OF RUNNING THEIR COLONIES. VIRGINIA, FOR EXAMPLE, HAD A GOVERNOR AND ELECTED REPRESENTATIVES. MARYLAND LET ONLY LANDOWNERS VOTE. NEW YORK USUALLY HAD ONE LEADER WHO MADE MOST OF THE DECISIONS FOR THE COLONY.

TO FORM THESE COLONIES INTO A SINGLE NATION, HOWEVER, COLONIAL LEADERS HAD TO FIRST DECIDE ON ONE FORM OF GOVERNMENT. EACH COLONY EXCEPT GEORGIA SENT REPRESENTATIVES TO THE FIRST CONTINENTAL CONGRESS. THERE, THEY AGREED THAT THEY WANTED TO BE ONE NATION, SEPARATE FROM ENGLAND.

King George ignored it. Many people realized that the only way America could break away from British rule would be to fight. In Philadelphia and many other cities, men began gathering weapons and training to fight. John Ross was among them.

Ross and men like him became known as minutemen. They were regular citizens who had not been part of a formal army. But they trained after work so that they could be "ready in a minute" if called to action. Most were young men. Every small village or settlement had its own unit of minutemen.

The minutemen soon had to put down their rakes and aprons and pick up their guns. The American Revolutionary War began on April 19, 1775, in Lexington, Massachusetts. The minutemen had clashed with British troops on a road just outside of Boston.

British soldiers were not in Philadelphia yet, but everyone knew they were coming. Betsy and John worried, but they had to keep working.

They made chairs and curtains, they sewed
tablecloths for a wedding. But after work each day,
John trained with the minutemen.

Early in 1776, John was badly injured. No
one is really sure what happened. He may have
been hurt by exploding gunpowder that blew up
while he was on guard duty. Another version of
events says simply that he was hurt while training.
It *is* certain that John died of his injuries, and
on January 21, 1776,
he was buried in
Philadelphia.

Betsy Ross was
just twenty-four
years old. In the
middle of a war,
separated from
her faith and her
family, she was
now a widow, too.

Chapter 4
A New Flag

To pay off money that John owed when he died, Betsy had to close his shop. Several months later, she bravely opened one of her own. It would not be easy to run a business alone. She had to find new customers, pay the bills, and order supplies. She had to do all the sewing work herself. But Betsy had watched her great-aunt Sarah run her business, so she thought she could do it, too.

The war turned out to be good news for Betsy's business. As people in Philadelphia prepared to fight, they needed the very things she was good at making. Soldiers needed blankets and bedding. Armies needed cots and tents. And everyone needed flags.

Each unit of the growing colonial army required its own flag. Each colony had its own flag, too. Even ships flew flags. They were all different, and each had to be made by hand.

Betsy's sewing skills were perfect for this job. The flags had to look great, but they also had to be sturdy to wave in any weather.

In the spring of 1776, there was not one flag to represent all the colonies. Several different flags had been used by American troops in battles. Most had taken parts of the British flag, which was red, white, and blue.

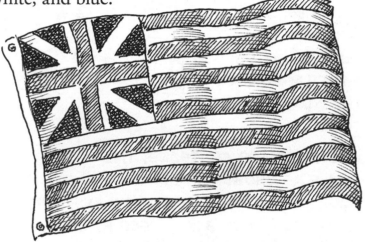

Some of the leaders of the colonies wanted what they were starting to call the United States to have a flag all its own, one that everyone could rally behind.

EARLY COLONIAL FLAGS

COLONIES HAD THEIR OWN FLAGS, BUT MOST ALSO USED THE FLAG OF GREAT BRITAIN, KNOWN AS THE UNION JACK. DURING THE REVOLUTIONARY WAR, HOWEVER, NEW FLAG DESIGNS WERE CREATED TO SUPPORT THE CAUSE OF LIBERTY.

CULPEPER MINUTEMEN, 1775

FLOWN BY CITIZEN-SOLDIERS IN VIRGINIA. IT SHOWED A RATTLESNAKE AND THE WORDS "DON'T TREAD ON ME."

WASHINGTON'S CRUISERS, 1775

THIS FLAG SHOWED A PINE TREE, WHICH WAS POPULAR ON FLAGS IN NEW ENGLAND. IT WAS FLOWN ON BOATS USED BY GEORGE WASHINGTON. AROUND THE TREE IT READ "AN APPEAL TO HEAVEN."

GRAND UNION, 1775

WASHINGTON HELPED DESIGN THIS FLAG, WHICH INCLUDED THE UNION JACK IN THE CORNER, BUT ALSO HAD THE NOW-FAMILIAR THIRTEEN RED AND WHITE STRIPES.

WASHINGTON'S PERSONAL FLAG
A BLUE FLAG WITH THIRTEEN SIX-POINTED
WHITE STARS FLEW OVER WASHINGTON'S
CAMPS THROUGHOUT THE WAR.

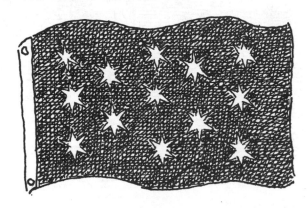

BUNKER HILL FLAG, 1775
ALL RED EXCEPT FOR A PINE TREE ON THE
UPPER LEFT, THE FLAG WAS FIRST FLOWN
DURING THE BATTLE OF BUNKER HILL IN 1775.

There's a great American legend that Betsy Ross
sewed the very first American flag. Is it true? Her
family says so! It's a story that's become a part of
the country's early history.

Nearly one hundred years after the beginning
of the Revolutionary War, Betsy's family told this
story: Three men visited Betsy at her Philadelphia
shop. One was George Ross, John's uncle.

He knew Betsy and was aware of her skill at sewing. George Ross had been part of the First Continental Congress and a leader in the colonies. The second man was another colonial leader, Robert Morris. He was a very rich man who helped raise money to pay for the colonists' fight. The third man, according to the story, was George Washington.

GEORGE WASHINGTON

BORN IN VIRGINIA IN
1732, GEORGE WASHINGTON
EXPECTED TO ENJOY A LIFE
AS A GENTLEMAN FARMER. HIS
LEADERSHIP SKILLS AND HIS
BELIEF IN FREEDOM LED HIM
ON A VERY DIFFERENT PATH.

AFTER WORKING AS A
SURVEYOR IN THE LANDS THAT
BRITAIN HOPED TO ADD TO ITS VIRGINIA COLONY,
WASHINGTON SERVED IN THE BRITISH ARMY. HE
FOUGHT IN A WAR AGAINST FRENCH SETTLERS
FROM CANADA. AFTER THAT WAR, HE RETURNED TO
LIFE ON HIS LARGE FARM, BUT GREW TROUBLED
BY WHAT BRITAIN WAS DOING TO ITS COLONIES.
HE JOINED THE ASSEMBLY IN VIRGINIA AND WAS
SENT TO THE FIRST CONTINENTAL CONGRESS. HIS
MILITARY EXPERIENCE MADE HIM THE NATURAL
CHOICE TO LEAD THE NEW CONTINENTAL ARMY.

GENERAL WASHINGTON LED THE ARMY
THROUGHOUT THE REVOLUTIONARY WAR. HE MADE
BOLD DECISIONS AND TURNED A MOTLEY CREW OF
COLONIAL SOLDIERS INTO A WINNING ARMY. IT
TOOK SIX YEARS, BUT THE AMERICANS DEFEATED
A LARGER BRITISH FORCE AND WON THE WAR.

THE TREATY THAT OFFICIALLY ENDED THE CONFLICT
WAS SIGNED IN 1783.

HAILED AS A NATIONAL HERO, WASHINGTON
BECAME THE COUNTRY'S FIRST PRESIDENT IN 1789.
THE SAME STRONG LEADERSHIP AND BELIEF IN
FREEDOM THAT HAD MADE HIM A GREAT GENERAL
HELPED HIM ORGANIZE THE MANY DIFFERENT PARTS
OF THE NEW NATION. WORKING WITH CONGRESS,
HE FORMED THE LAWS AND STRUCTURES THAT STILL
GOVERN THE NATION.

AFTER TWO TERMS AS PRESIDENT, HE LEFT
OFFICE IN 1797. WASHINGTON DIED TWO YEARS
LATER, BUT REMAINS THE "FATHER OF OUR COUNTRY."

In 1776, Washington was the leader of the new Continental army. When they visited Betsy's shop, the three men brought a sketch of a flag. They needed to have a sample made. Betsy showed them a few ways to make it better. The men had drawn a square flag. Betsy told them that the flag should be longer. Their sketch showed thirteen red and white stripes. There was one stripe for each of the thirteen colonies. Betsy showed them how she could sew those stripes together.

A blue square in the upper left corner had stars. The stars each had six points. Betsy looked at the stars and realized she had a better way. She folded a piece of paper eight times, made one snip with her scissors, and showed the men a five-pointed star. Betsy said that making stars this way would be faster and easier.

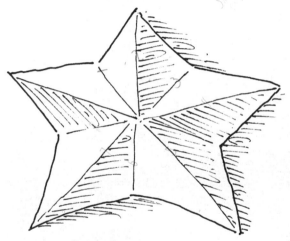

Washington and the other men liked what she showed them. They left Betsy with some money to buy fabric. They asked her to make a sample of this new flag to show Congress.

While Betsy worked on her flag, the
Continental Congress was debating the terms
of the Declaration of Independence.

The leaders of the colonies said that no nation should rule another. They wrote that "all men are created equal," and that no one could take away their rights to "life, liberty, and the pursuit of happiness." The Declaration listed the many things that King George and Great Britain had done to the colonies. It ended by "declaring" that the colonies "are free and independent states."

The Declaration was approved on July 4, 1776, which is now known as Independence Day. Copies were carried throughout the colonies and read to bigger and bigger crowds of people. Four days later, Betsy was probably among the thousands who heard it read out loud on the streets of Philadelphia.

A year later, on June 14, 1777, Congress passed a law that the flag of the new United States would look like the one described in the story about Betsy Ross. But did she really sew that first flag?

Historians have found no evidence to support the family's story. Although there is no concrete proof, Betsy *did* spend many of the rest of her working years making flags, many of which were indeed the Stars and Stripes.

Chapter 5
A Hometown Invaded

By the winter of 1776, the Continental army had lost battles in New York and retreated south into New Jersey. Unless the battling colonists could stop the British, Philadelphia would soon be under attack, as well. General Washington came up with a daring plan. He knew that Hessians, German troops hired by Britain, were camping near Trenton, New Jersey. Many people believed they would soon head to Philadelphia.

On December 26, 1776, Washington gathered some of his troops near McKonkey's Ferry, Pennsylvania. (The site is known today as Washington Crossing.) Quietly climbing into boats, they sneaked across the icy Delaware River at

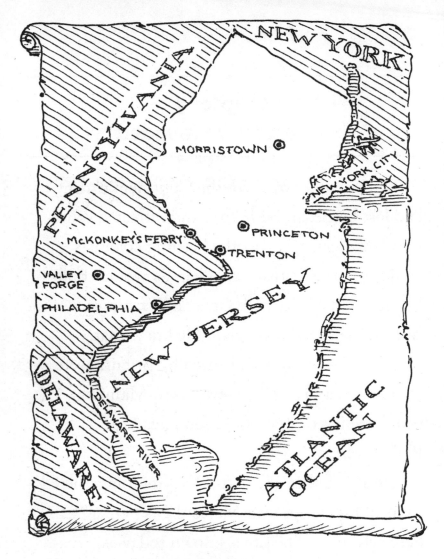

night. They arrived at the Hessians' camp during a
Christmas party and quickly defeated them.

Washington and his men went on to win an important battle at Princeton, New Jersey. They camped for the winter in Morristown, New Jersey, about eighty miles to the north of Philadelphia. But the war was still moving closer to that key city.

PAINTING OF A LEGEND

IN 1851, A GERMAN PAINTER NAMED EMANUEL LEUTZE MADE A FAMOUS PAINTING OF WASHINGTON CROSSING THE DELAWARE RIVER. IT'S ONE OF THE MOST WELL-KNOWN IMAGES IN AMERICAN HISTORY. THE PAINTER IMAGINED WASHINGTON STANDING IN A ROWBOAT. AROUND HIM, MEN WORKED HARD TO ROW THE BOAT THROUGH THE ICY WATERS. IN THE BACKGROUND, A HORSE STOOD IN ANOTHER BOAT.

BUT LEUTZE HAD MANY DETAILS WRONG. THE CROSSING WAS IN THE DARK OF NIGHT, NOT DAYTIME. THE WEATHER WAS NOT CLEAR, BUT RAINY. DURING THE ACTUAL CROSSING, ALL THE MEN WOULD BE STANDING, NOT JUST WASHINGTON.

FUTURE PRESIDENT JAMES MONROE IS SHOWN
IN THE BOAT WITH WASHINGTON, BUT HE DID NOT
CROSS UNTIL LATER. A BLACK SOLDIER NAMED
PRINCE WHIPPLE IS SHOWN IN THE BOAT, BUT HE
WAS NOT REALLY WITH THE ARMY THAT DAY.

THOUGH MANY OF THE DETAILS MAY NOT BE
CORRECT, THE STORY WAS TRUE. WASHINGTON'S
BRAVE RIDE ACROSS THE RIVER ON A DECEMBER
NIGHT IN 1776 HELPED TURN THE TIDE OF THE
REVOLUTIONARY WAR.

Back in Philadelphia, Betsy's life was changing again. She had met a sailor named Joseph Ashburn. On June 15, 1777, Betsy Ross became Betsy Ashburn when the pair married at the Old Swedes' Church in Philadelphia.

Betsy continued to be busy at work. That spring, she was paid fourteen pounds and twelve shillings (about $2,600) for Pennsylvania ship flags, known as *colors*. One of those flags was flown aboard a ship called the *Hetty*. Joseph had joined the ship's crew not long after their wedding.

Just three weeks after Ashburn married Betsy, his ship headed out as part of the young American navy. One of the first battles he fought was near Brandywine Creek, just west of Philadelphia.

The colonial troops lost the Battle of Brandywine. That opened the way for British troops to move toward and capture Philadelphia. Thousands of citizens fled to the countryside and safety. Betsy decided to stay. She had a business to run.

On September 26, 1777, led by Lord Cornwallis and General William Howe, the British advanced into the city. Row after row of red-coated soldiers marched through the streets as Betsy and her neighbors looked on. The army band played, but no one sang along. The soldiers moved into the city's buildings and filled city parks. The officers took control of the fancy homes of some of the wealthier residents. The British even camped in the same building where Congress had met! They tore out walls to make the first floor into housing for troops. They put beds on the second floor to care for wounded American prisoners.

A week later, Washington tried to attack British forces staying outside the city near Germantown. But the colonial army was beaten back. Wounded soldiers from both sides were carried the six miles back to Philadelphia. Betsy was among the many women who helped take care of the men. They rolled bandages and sewed slings and blankets.

THE ROYAL NAVY

WHEN THE AMERICAN REVOLUTION BEGAN, GREAT BRITAIN HAD THE LARGEST NAVY IN THE WORLD. IT HAD RULED THE WORLD'S OCEANS FOR ALMOST ONE HUNDRED FIFTY YEARS. THE ROYAL NAVY HAD MORE THAN ONE HUNDRED THIRTY LARGE BATTLESHIPS AND THOUSANDS MORE SMALLER BOATS. THE AMERICAN NAVY WAS BRAND-NEW. IT HAD ONLY A HANDFUL OF SMALL SHIPS, AND MOST OF THEM COULD NOT SAFELY SAIL FAR FROM LAND.

BRITAIN USED ITS SHIPS TO CARRY SOLDIERS
AND SUPPLIES TO AMERICA. IN 1776, AN INVASION
FORCE ARRIVED IN NEW YORK HARBOR, CARRYING
MORE THAN TWELVE THOUSAND TROOPS. BRITISH
SHIPS BOMBED COASTAL CITIES, AND TRIED TO
PREVENT SUPPLIES FROM REACHING PLACES SUCH
AS BOSTON OR CHARLESTON.

BUT THE MAIN BATTLES OF THE WAR WERE
FOUGHT ON LAND, NOT SEA. AND FRENCH SHIPS
ENTERED THE WAR ON AMERICA'S SIDE IN 1778,
WHICH EVENED THE ODDS. IN THE END, THE
BRITISH NAVY WAS NOT STRONG ENOUGH TO
TURN THE TIDE OF THE WAR.

Not long after this defeat, Washington made
camp for the winter and spring at Valley Forge,
Pennsylvania. For seven months, his troops
suffered there with little food or shelter. Even
though Philadelphia was only twenty miles away,
British troops blocked any help from reaching
Washington and his men. Betsy and other
patriots made clothing and tents for the men.

The clothes, food, and other supplies were sneaked out of the city and quietly transported to the starving soldiers.

During this time, Betsy did not know where her new husband was. His ship had not come back to Philadelphia yet. There was no way for him to get word to her. She did not know if he was even alive.

VALLEY FORGE

THE TWELVE THOUSAND CONTINENTAL SOLDIERS WHO CAMPED AT VALLEY FORGE IN THE WINTER OF 1777-78 SUFFERED GREATLY. THEY DID NOT HAVE ENOUGH FOOD OR CLOTHING. SOME DIDN'T EVEN HAVE SHOES. THEY HAD TO LIVE IN TENTS OR SMALL WOODEN HUTS WITH DIRT FLOORS. MORE THAN TWO THOUSAND OF THEM DIED FROM COLD, HUNGER, OR DISEASE.

EVEN THOUGH NO BATTLE WAS EVER FOUGHT THERE, VALLEY FORGE BECAME ONE OF THE MOST IMPORTANT SITES IN THE AMERICAN REVOLUTION.

BY SURVIVING TOGETHER, THE AMERICAN ARMY BECAME STRONGER. THEY SAW THEIR LEADER, GEORGE WASHINGTON, LIVING IN THE CAMP WITH THEM. THEY GAINED STRENGTH FROM WHAT THEY LEARNED ABOUT ONE ANOTHER. THEY USED THEIR TIME IN THE SPRING TO PRACTICE AND DRILL AND TRAIN. THEY LEFT VALLEY FORGE UNITED AND READY TO BATTLE TO THE END.

IF VALLEY FORGE WAS A TEST, THE AMERICAN ARMY PASSED WITH FLYING COLORS.

Chapter 6
Victory . . . and a New Life

By the spring of 1778, the British had left
Philadelphia. Part of their army headed out to
attack colonies to the south. The rest of the
British moved on to New York City, where the
fighting was fierce. In Philadelphia, they left
behind a huge mess. Many buildings were ruined,
most of the food in the city was gone, and ships in
the port had been burned.

The British army had taken furniture, horses, and wagons. Thousands of Pennsylvania residents left with the British, choosing to side with England over the new nation of America. Betsy and her neighbors lived and worked in a city where it became harder and harder to survive.

Amid all the chaos, Joseph Ashburn returned safely from his latest voyage. While he and other men worked hard to clean up the mess the British had left behind, Betsy kept sewing.

Along with flags, she sewed military supplies
for the Continental army. Colonial soldiers used
long-barreled guns called *muskets*. To load one,
a soldier poured gunpowder down the barrel.
Then he stuffed a lead ball in after it. Soldiers
carried the powder and the balls in small bags
called *cartridges*. Betsy and other women sewed
thousands of canvas cartridges.

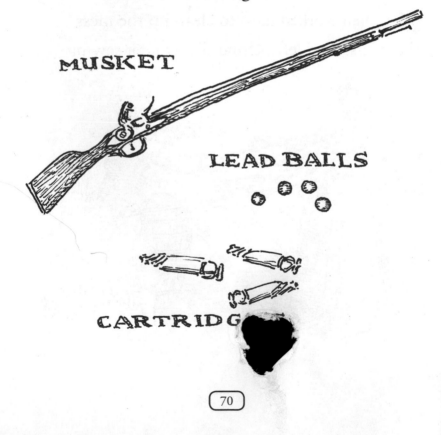

MUSKET

LEAD BALLS

CARTRIDG

Betsy and Joseph's first child, a daughter named Aucilla, was born on September 15, 1779. Food was still scarce in the city. People were burning furniture to keep warm. Sadly, Aucilla got sick and died when she was less than a year old. In 1781, the couple had a second daughter, Eliza.

Later that same year, Joseph set sail on the *Lion*, which went all the way to Europe, chasing British ships. The *Lion* was captured, and Joseph was put in a British prison called the Old Mill.

OLD MILL PRISON

The Old Mill Prison was a terrible place, with too many men packed into too little space. The prisoners actually sold their clothes to buy bread to eat. Disease spread quickly among the men. Joseph was among the hundreds of men who died there. Betsy Ross Ashburn was a widow once again.

She heard the news about her husband's death weeks later from an old friend. John Claypoole had known Betsy since they were children. He had later become a sailor and had ended up as

a prisoner in the Old Mill along with Joseph
Ashburn. As a friend, he wanted to give Betsy
the sad news in person. When he made it back to
Philadelphia, he visited her straightaway.

Losing yet another husband was very sad,
but Betsy had some reasons to be happy. Her
daughter Eliza was healthy. She was busy with
her work. And the American Revolution had
ended! After a series of battles in 1780 and 1781,

Washington's forces trapped the British on a peninsula in Yorktown, Virginia. French ships joined the fight and prevented British ships from rescuing their soldiers. Stuck in this trap, British general Cornwallis surrendered his army to Washington in October 1781. The Americans had won!

Two years later, Betsy's old friend John
Claypoole asked her to be his wife. They were
married on May 8, 1783. Betsy had a new
husband and a new partner in the upholstery and
flag-making business. John left the sea to help
make their business grow.

Chapter 7
The Claypooles Move Ahead

During the war, people in the Society of Friends had a difficult time. They wanted to support their neighbors, but they were against war or fighting of any kind. They did not serve in the army for either the British or the American colonies. Some of these Quakers, however, did want to fight and support the cause of freedom. During the war, they chose to leave the main body of the Society and form the Free Quakers. The new group stuck to their beliefs of plain talk and dress, and of looking to their inner light. However, they also saw that sometimes fighting for what was right was okay.

After marrying, Betsy and John joined this new group. They began attending services in a building the group had built in 1783. Betsy was able to return to her Quaker roots and to the services she had grown up with.

FREE QUAKER MEETINGHOUSE

While Betsy was returning to her Quaker family, she and John were starting their own. In 1785, their first daughter, Clarissa, was born. She was joined a year later by Susan. The Claypooles continued to work together in their shop, moving to a larger home in 1787. They needed the room; by then, they had two more daughters, Rachel and Jane.

Betsy's life was busy with work and five daughters to care for. At the shop, business was good. Along with flags and home furnishings, they made furniture for ships. John knew exactly what types of things ships needed, and he was able to bring in more customers. In fact, the shop did well enough that John and Betsy could afford to buy a horse and carriage by 1786.

When he was not working, John spent time helping others. The Quakers had always been antislavery. Inspired by his Quaker beliefs, John worked with groups that tried to free slaves and aid prisoners. These new groups sought to make sure free black people remained free and were not kidnapped back into slavery. They visited jails and demanded fair and healthy treatment for the prisoners.

By 1793, Betsy and John had a fine family, a good home, and steady work. But in the summer of that year, a tragic epidemic spread throughout Philadelphia. Yellow fever struck, and thousands of people died from the disease. Betsy's parents died early in the epidemic. Betsy's sister Deborah died, too. Her sister Mary died soon after, also possibly from the fever.

The yellow fever epidemic was over by early 1794. That year, John found another job. He went to work for the new United States government as a customs inspector. His job was to check the imported items brought to Philadelphia on ships.

AREA WITH MOST DEATHS

THE SPREAD OF YELLOW FEVER IN PHILADELPHIA 1793

Betsy continued running their shop, which
was making furniture for the new government
buildings. Philadelphia had been chosen as the
capital of the young United States (though the
capital would later move to New York City and
then Washington, DC). Experts such as Betsy
made cushions, pillows, wall coverings, curtains,
and more.

YELLOW FEVER

YELLOW FEVER IS A SERIOUS INFECTION
THAT CAUSES HIGH FEVERS, YELLOWISH SKIN,
HEADACHES, AND NAUSEA. IT CAN BE QUITE DEADLY.
WHEN IT STRUCK PHILADELPHIA IN AUGUST 1793,
IT SPREAD RAPIDLY. THERE WAS NO CURE, THOUGH
DOCTORS TRIED MAKING PATIENTS BREATHE
SMOKE, DRINK COFFEE AND VINEGAR, OR BLEED.
NOTHING WORKED, AND BY THE TIME THE EPIDEMIC
WAS OVER, MORE THAN FIVE THOUSAND PEOPLE

HAD DIED. MORE THAN TWENTY THOUSAND MORE HAD EVACUATED THE CITY, TRYING TO ESCAPE THE DISEASE.

THOUGH PEOPLE DID NOT KNOW IT AT THE TIME, YELLOW FEVER IS SPREAD BY MOSQUITOES, WHICH COME OUT IN THE HEAT OF SUMMER. WHEN THE COLD WEATHER ARRIVED IN NOVEMBER, THE MOSQUITOES DIED OUT, AND THE EPIDEMIC FINALLY ENDED.

Congress met in Philadelphia, and George
Washington, the leader of the Continental army,
had been elected as the first president of the new
nation. His office was in Philadelphia, too.

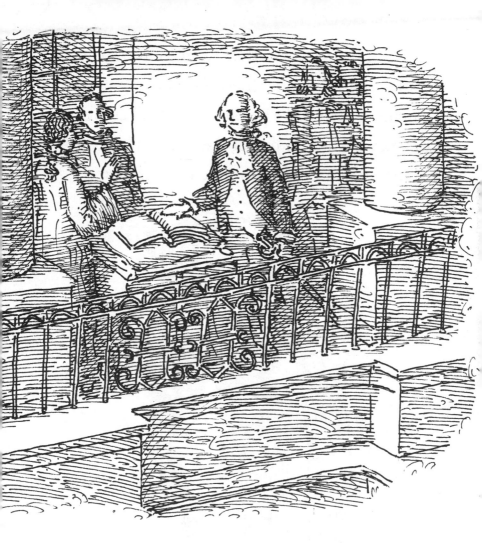

The city became the center of activity for those
who took on the difficult work of turning thirteen
colonies into a united nation.

With their success, Betsy and John Claypoole could afford a grander lifestyle. The Claypoole daughters attended a private school. They went to fancy parties. At one of them, Betsy's niece Margaret danced with President Washington himself.

Betsy Griscom Ross Ashburn Claypoole had come a long way from struggling to find food during the cold winters of war.

Chapter 8
Busy to the End

The end of the 1700s
was a time of more change
for America, and for
Betsy and her family.
In 1795, she and John
had another daughter,
Harriet, but the baby
died ten months
later. In 1799, Eliza
Ashburn, Betsy's oldest
daughter, married a
ship's captain. And
later that year, George
Washington passed away
at the age of sixty-seven.

Washington's death saddened the entire nation that he had helped create. In Philadelphia, numerous public services and funerals were held to honor him. Betsy and her family took part, joining thousands of citizens.

In 1800, John Claypoole suffered what was probably a stroke. He could no longer work. He stayed home—and usually in bed—for the rest of his life. Betsy did her best to care for him, but it was not easy. By 1803, they were receiving money as charity from the Free Quakers to help pay their bills.

Betsy kept working. Her daughters helped as much as they could, but one by one, they married and started their own families. Betsy enjoyed being a grandmother. One of Clarissa's twins was named for her!

Betsy continued making flags. The short War of 1812 between America and Great Britain led to more orders from the US Army and Navy.

In 1817, John Claypoole died at home. Betsy
had worked hard to care for him, even as she grew
older herself. For the third time in her life, Betsy
was a widow.

Ten years later, at age seventy-five, Betsy finally
stopped working. Her daughter Clarissa, and
Margaret, Betsy's niece, took over the shop. Betsy
left Philadelphia to live with her daughter Susan
in the countryside of Abington, Pennsylvania.
She made regular trips back to the big city to go
to Free Quaker meetings and to see old friends.

Philadelphia continued to grow. When Betsy was born, about twenty-five thousand people lived there. By the 1830 census, Philadelphia was home to more than eighty thousand!

In July 1835, America turned fifty-nine years old. As always on Independence Day, US flags flew everywhere. That year, there were twenty-four stars on the flag.

In 1835, Betsy moved back to Philadelphia to live with her daughter Jane. On January 30, 1836, when she was eighty-four years old, Betsy Ross passed away. Jane's son, William Canby, remembered that when she died, she was "beloved and respected by all who had ever known her."

Chapter 9
A Legend Is Born

The story of Betsy Ross might have ended with her death in 1836 if not for William Canby. William was Betsy's grandson. In 1870, he

gave a speech in Philadelphia to the Historical Society of Pennsylvania. William had gathered memories of Betsy from his family to share with the group. In his speech, Canby said that Betsy Ross had made the first US flag.

"This lady is the one to whom belongs the honor of having made with her own hands the first flag," Canby said. He said that Betsy's daughters remembered hearing the story from their mother. He had even spoken to Betsy's niece Margaret.

Canby's story caught the public's attention. Not long after, in 1876, America celebrated its one hundredth birthday. Patriotic speeches like Canby's were widely repeated. People were very interested in the details of how the United States had gained its independence. The story of the "first flag" was soon told all over the country.

By the 1890s, the story of Betsy Ross was so popular that the city of Philadelphia wanted to create a way to remember her. One of the houses that she *might* have lived in was still standing. It became a tourist attraction. The people who lived there hung a sign that said "First Flag of the US Made in This House." In 1898, it was established as the American Flag House. The house became a museum dedicated to the life of Betsy Ross and the story of Philadelphia.

In the years since Canby's speech, historians have tried to learn more about Betsy Ross. They have found no direct evidence that she did in fact sew the first flag. Washington's papers do not mention her. Congressional records do not mention her. Historians require more proof than stories and memories. However, Betsy was part

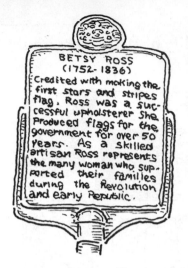

BETSY ROSS
(1752-1836)
Credited with making the first stars and stripes flag. Ross was a successful upholsterer. She produced flags for the government for over 50 years. As a skilled artisan Ross represents the many women who supported their families during the Revolution and early Republic.

of an amazing time in American history. The story of her life, her work, and her family remains true, even if the reason she is famous may not be.

Today, more than 250,000 people visit the Betsy Ross House in Philadelphia, Pennsylvania, each year. It is located a few blocks from Independence Hall and the Liberty Bell, and it remains one of the most visited sites in the city.

BETSY ROSS HOUSE →
CHRIST CHURCH →
INDEPENDENCE HALL ↑
OLD SWEDES' CHURCH →
ELFRETH'S ALLEY ↓

FLAG ETIQUETTE

THE UNITED STATES FLAG CODE HAS MANY RULES ABOUT THE PROPER USE AND TREATMENT OF THE AMERICAN FLAG. THESE ARE DESIGNED TO MAKE SURE THAT THE FLAG ALWAYS RECEIVES THE RESPECT IT DESERVES. AS A SYMBOL OF THE NATION, IT IS MORE THAN JUST A PIECE OF CLOTH.

* FLAGS SHOULD BE FLOWN ONLY DURING DAYLIGHT HOURS AND NEVER IN THE RAIN.

* WHEN DISPLAYED WITH STATE FLAGS, THE US FLAG SHOULD BE HIGHEST.

* A FLAG IS FLOWN AT HALF-STAFF, OR ONLY HALFWAY UP A POLE, TO HONOR THE PASSING OF AN IMPORTANT PERSON.

* WHEN THE FLAG IS HUNG ON A WALL, THE BLUE FIELD SHOULD ALWAYS BE ON THE LEFT.

THE AMERICAN FLAG

TODAY, THE FLAG HAS FIFTY STARS AND THIRTEEN STRIPES. BUT IT HAS GONE THROUGH A FEW CHANGES OVER THE DECADES.

* * *

THE "BETSY ROSS" HAD THIRTEEN STARS IN A CIRCLE ON THE BLUE AREA, WHICH IS CALLED A *CANTON*. IT WAS MADE THE OFFICIAL FLAG OF THE UNITED STATES ON JUNE 14, 1777. THAT DAY IS STILL CELEBRATED AS FLAG DAY.

* * *

IN 1795, TWO MORE STARS AND TWO MORE STRIPES WERE ADDED TO THE FLAG FOR KENTUCKY AND VERMONT. IT WAS THE ONLY OFFICIAL US FLAG WITH MORE THAN THIRTEEN STRIPES.

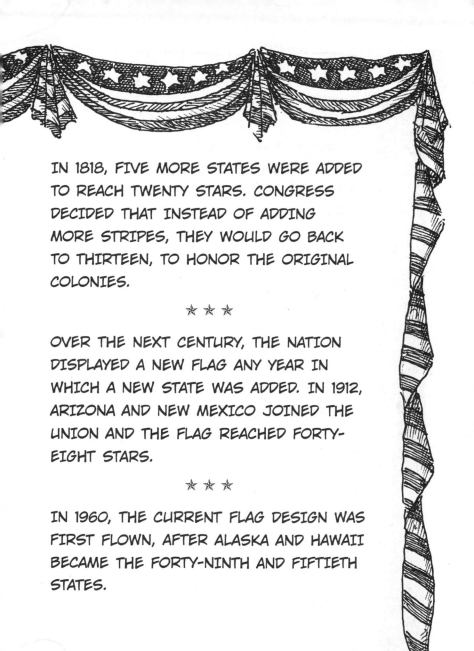

IN 1818, FIVE MORE STATES WERE ADDED TO REACH TWENTY STARS. CONGRESS DECIDED THAT INSTEAD OF ADDING MORE STRIPES, THEY WOULD GO BACK TO THIRTEEN, TO HONOR THE ORIGINAL COLONIES.

⭐ ⭐ ⭐

OVER THE NEXT CENTURY, THE NATION DISPLAYED A NEW FLAG ANY YEAR IN WHICH A NEW STATE WAS ADDED. IN 1912, ARIZONA AND NEW MEXICO JOINED THE UNION AND THE FLAG REACHED FORTY-EIGHT STARS.

⭐ ⭐ ⭐

IN 1960, THE CURRENT FLAG DESIGN WAS FIRST FLOWN, AFTER ALASKA AND HAWAII BECAME THE FORTY-NINTH AND FIFTIETH STATES.

TIMELINE OF
BETSY ROSS'S LIFE

1752 — Born on January 1 near Philadelphia

1764 — Starts work at John Webster's shop

1773 — Marries fellow worker John Ross

1776 — John Ross dies from injuries
Betsy Ross is visited by George Washington
and asked to make the US flag

1777 — Betsy marries Joseph Ashburn

1779 — Daughter Aucilla born and dies

1781 — Daughter Eliza born

1782 — Joseph Ashburn dies in the Old Mill prison in England

1783 — Betsy marries John Claypoole

1785 — Clarissa, first of five Claypoole children, born

1817 — John Claypoole dies

1827 — Betsy retires

1836 — Betsy Ross dies in Philadelphia at age eighty-four

TIMELINE OF
THE WORLD

French and Indian War ends; solidifies British control of America	1763
Stamp Act passed by Parliament James Watt perfects the steam engine	1765
Revolutionary War begins	1775
Declaration of Independence approved	1776
British captain James Cook "discovers" Hawaii	1778
America wins final land battle of the Revolutionary War	1781
US Constitution approved	1787
French Revolution begins George Washington elected first president	1789
United States makes Louisiana Purchase from France	1803
Napoleon proclaims himself emperor of France Lewis and Clark expedition to the West begins	1804
The War of 1812 between Britain and America begins	1812
Napoleon finally defeated at Battle of Waterloo	1815
First railroad to carry passengers opens in England	1825
Victoria becomes queen of the United Kingdom of Great Britain and Ireland; she rules for sixty-three years until 1901	1837

BIBLIOGRAPHY

* Hakim, Joy. **A History of US: From Colonies to Country: 1735–1791**. New York: Oxford University Press, 1993.

* Miller, Marla. **Betsy Ross and the Making of America.** New York: Henry Holt and Co., 2010.

* Roop, Peter and Connie. **In Their Own Words: Betsy Ross**. New York: Scholastic, 2001.

* Books for young readers

ONLINE RESOURCES

Website of the Betsy Ross house and museum in Philadelphia:
www.historicphiladelphia.org/betsy-ross-house/what-to-see/

The complete text of Canby's 1870 speech:
www.ushistory.org/betsy/more/canby.htm

A detailed site of the story of Betsy Ross and the
investigation into the history of the flag:
www.ushistory.org/betsy/index.html